PRINCIPLES OF COMMUNICATION IN THE SOCIAL CARE SETTING

Level 2 and 3

This is a learning workbook to accompany the Certificate and Diploma in Health and Social Care

Maria Eales
1/1/2013

ISBN-13:
978-1491221594

ISBN-10:
1491221593

WHY DO WE COMMUNICATE?

There are any reasons people we communicate but these reasons can be split into four main groups.

Share	• Share ideas, news, information and opinions
Express Needs	• To ask for things they need, to tell people they are happy sad, in pain.
Give instructions	• Tell people what to do, describe how to do something. Teach others about something.
Answer and ask questions	• To answer and ask questions, gain information, learn things.

ACTIVITY 1

Think of three other reasons why you communicate that are not included in the list above.

_____

_____

_____

_____

_____

_____

EFFECTIVE COMMUNICATION

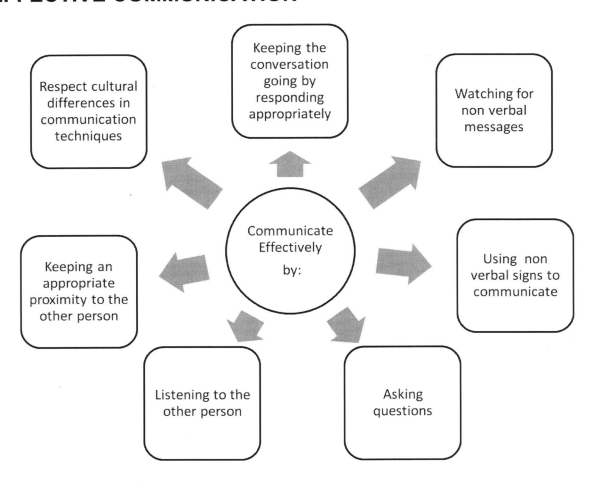

Maintaining effective communication requires different skills. This included using both verbal and non-verbal communication.

Verbal communication involves speaking, listening and then answering the person when they reply. Non-verbal communication involves making appropriate facial expressions, using body language, such as nodding your head and using hand gestures at appropriate times.

Sometimes, you will need to keep the conversation going by asking open questions to facilitate a detailed answer from the other person.

At all times you should be watching the other person's facial expressions as well as listening to what they are saying.

Make sure that you summarise the conversation at intervals to ensure that they understand what you are saying and to check that you understand what they are trying to communicate.

WHY IS GOOD COMMUNICATION IMPORTANT?

In the health and social care setting, the professional and the client must build a trusting relationship. Good communication helps this to happen. When the health and social care profession uses effective communication, they can find out everything they need to know about their client.

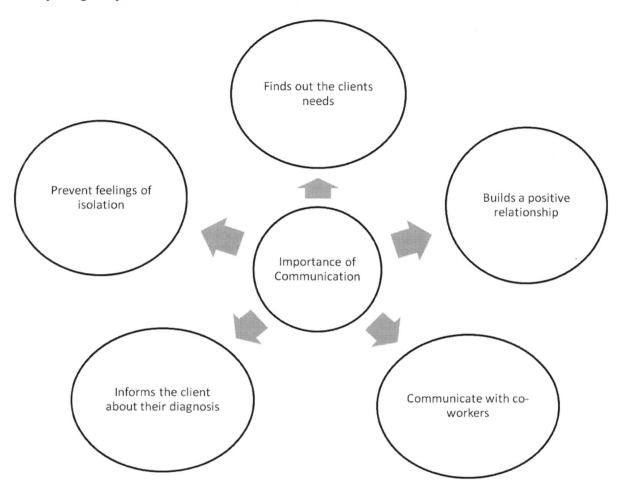

ACTIVITY 2

LET'S TALK ABOUT IT

Make a list of all the reasons why would need to communicate with a client.

_____

_____

_____

FORMS OF COMMUNICATION

Let's look at the different forms of communication on a bit more detail..

Verbal communication

Verbal communication uses words and tone of voice to pass information to another person. This information might be about feelings, thoughts desires or to pass on information that the other person needs.

Good verbal communication should involve a clear voce, appropriate tone and use words that the other person can understand. It also involves listening carefully to the other person to make sure they understand what you have said.

In the professional setting, it is important that you address the person in the way that they have requested. Don't naturally assume that you can use their first name or call them Mrs or Mr so and so. Always ask how a person likes to be addressed.

Non Verbal Communication

Seventy per cent of all communication is made using non-verbal communication methods. Very often, we are communicating and don't even realise it.

A teacher can stand at the front of a class of students and see who is bored, who's sad, happy or worried, just by looking at their body language and facial expressions.

It is the same with care professionals. They often watch their patients' body language to gain information about how they are feeling. If a person is in pain, it often shows on their face or they might hug there stomach or rub the part of their body that hurts.

If we are socialising with friends, the first indication that they are excited about something or worried about an issue, comes from their body language. We then use verbal communication to get the juicy details.

Look at the picture and describe how these people are feeling. Why do you think that they are feeling the way you have described?

This is an extreme form of non-verbal communication. If you compare your ideas to other class members, you will probably find that everyone else has described this situation in a similar way.

Stop and think for a moment on how you use non-verbal communication? Do you stroke your chin when you are deep in thought? Do you chew at your lip if you are worried? Ask friends or people who know you well if they have noticed any particular body language that you use on a regular basis.

ACTIVITY 3
ACTIONS SPEAK LOUDER THAN WORDS

In small groups, take it in turns to show an emotion or feeling to the rest of the group, using nothing but body language body language and facial expressions.

Here or some examples but you can also use your own ideas to try and catch your other classmates out!

- Pain
- Crying
- Happiness
- Laughter
- Anger
- Worried
- Thoughtful

ACTIVITY 4
WHAT DID YOU SAY?

This is an activity for pairs. Each of you thinks of five different things than you have at home. For example: a washing machine, hairdryer or puppy. Do not share your thoughts with the other person. Now you have to try and describe the items to the other person without saying what they are.

So, if you are thinking of a washing machine, you can't say 'washing machine' but you can describe the colour, shape, what it does, where it is etc.

ACTIVITY 5
WHAT'S THE SIGN?

For this task, you can either use the finger spelling chart of the next page or you can search for 'finger spelling' on the Internet.

Using nothing but finger spelling, have a short conversation with your class partner. Try and say something about yourself that they don't know.

Finger spelling is the easiest form of communication when speaking to a person who suffers with an auditory disability.

FINGER SPELLING ALPHABET

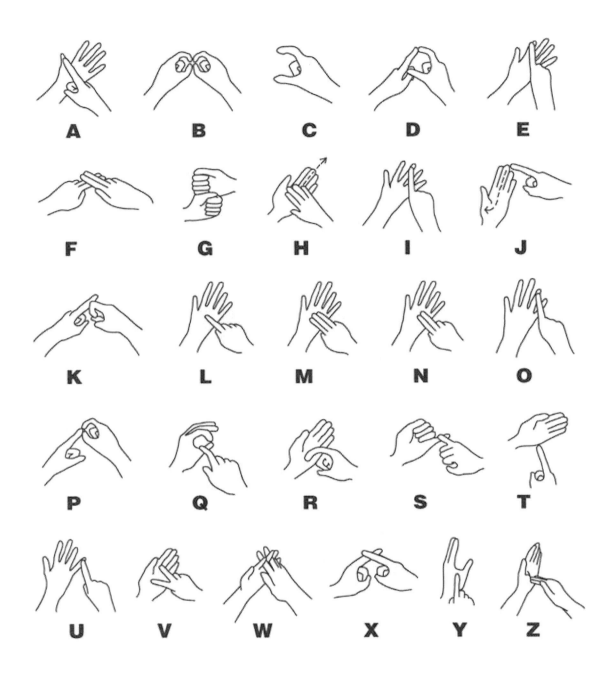

NOTES!

Please be aware that British Sign Language (BSL) finger spelling is different to the American version.

WEBSITE FOR BRITISH SIGN LANGUAGE

http://www.britishsignlanguage.com

You will find a complete guide to the alphabet demonstrated on this site.

ACTIVITY 6

THE BIG QUESTION

As a class, sit in a circle and one person has a small ball. Only the person holding the ball may speak. Once that person has made their point, they should throw the ball to another person across the circle. That person should then respond to the first person's point of view and add their own point of view.

The group can choose from one of the 'Big Questions' below or choose their own topic for discussion.

- Should people who miss hospital or doctors appoints be charged?
- Should people on benefits be made to do voluntary work?
- Do talent shows provide a platform to ridicule eccentric people?
- Should people with children be allowed to choose their holidays from work before people without children?
- Should children who do not pass five GCSEs at school be made to stay in education until they do?
- Should school uniforms be abolished?
- Should underage girls who get pregnant have their child adopted?

The exercise above allows debate without everyone speaking at once. It is very important that people are given a chance to say what they want to say without fear of ridicule. Listening to another person's point of view is a sign of respect. It doesn't mean that you have to agree with them but you must respect their right to have their own opinion.

Group communication is very important for anyone who works in the health and social care setting. However, it only works oif everyone is allowed to voice their opinion.

In most groups, there are those people who speak a lot and others who seldom speak. Talkative people can often dominate a conversation and it is up to the leader of the group discussion to make sure everyone has had the opportunity to speak. In the activity above, it is the ball that is managing the conversation because only the person holding the ball is allowed to say anything.

This system also forces people to listen to what is being said by others rather than just giving an opinion.

COMMUNICATION IN THE CARE SETTING

Communication is the care setting isn't just about speaking and listening to clients. There are far more communication methods that care professionals need to use to ensure that their needs are understood and met.

POINT TO CARDS

These can be used by people who have difficulty with speech and language. For example, people who have had a stroke that has taken their speech or people who don't speak English.

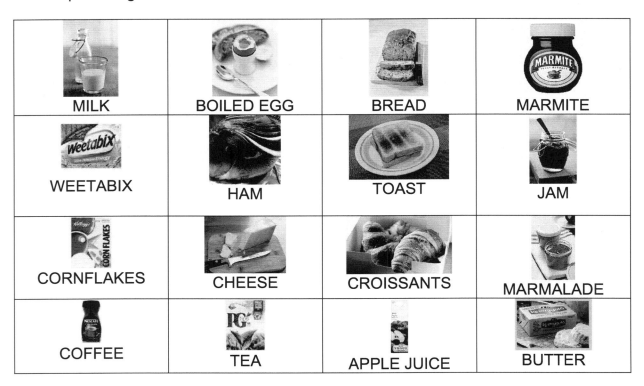

MILK	BOILED EGG	BREAD	MARMITE
WEETABIX	HAM	TOAST	JAM
CORNFLAKES	CHEESE	CROISSANTS	MARMALADE
COFFEE	TEA	APPLE JUICE	BUTTER

ACTIVITY 7

In pairs develop a 'Point Card' to help a client express their day to day needs. Do this on the computer if you can, so that it's easily readable.

You can use this in your portfolio as an example of non-verbal communication.

BRAILLE

This is a method of reading for people with visual impairment. The alphabet is written in clusters of raised bumps on the page. The visually impaired person runs their fingers over the bumps to read the sentences.

Each letter of the alphabet has a different cluster of bumps. You can see the Braille alphabet on the next page. In addition to the letters, there are also symbols for punctuation and joining words such as 'but' and 'and'.

BRAILLE ALPHABET

Uncontracted (Grade 1) Braille

a	b	c	d	e	f	g	h	i	j
k	l	m	n	o	p	q	r	s	t

u	v	x	y	z	w

You can easily make an example of a sentence in Braille by taking a piece of thick card and poking a thick need upwards to make the bumps. When you close your eyes and run your fingers over the bumps you will understand how hard it is to read Braille.

TEXTURED FLOOR SURFACES AND HANDRAILS
Often, hospitals and care homes have textured floor surfaces or hand rails so that visually impaired people know where they are.

Have you ever noticed the bobbled surface on the pavement by a pelican crossing? This is so that blind people know that they are at a crossing.

ELECTRONIC DEVICES
Mobile phones are now used by the majority of people, including health care professionals. They are used to co-ordinate emergency services and call for extra help if they need it. Text messages can be sent and received by people who have a hearing impairment.

Telephone amplifiers can make the ring tone of all telephones louder and they also amplify the sound of the person's voice on the other end of the line. There is also a system call a 'hearing loop'. This helps deaf people who use a hearing aid because it filters out all background noise and amplifies the sound. This system can also be used with a television to allow the deaf person to hear what the actors are saying without the background noise.

Door bells in people's homes can be fitted with a flashing light anywhere in the house. This means that a deaf person can 'see' when someone is at their door.

Obviously, we can't forget the computer and the advantages of emails for communicating with deaf people. However, there is also software available to convert text to speech for the visually impaired.

WRITTEN COMMUNICATION

This is very important to the work of any professional in the health and social care sector. Accurate record keeping is an essential skill and required good written communication skills.

A more formal style of writing is needed for keeping records on clients' progress, needs and condition. This is not the lace to use text message abbreviations and spellings.

ACTIVITY 8

Read the following reports that have been written into a client's notes and then rewrite the comments in a more appropriate way.

12/04/13

1. Maggie was a bit of a pain today. She kept shouting for her mother lol. Her chum came to visit but it didn't shut the old girl up
2. Harry doesn't no wot he wants 2 do b4 T so I just left him to watch tv in lounge.
3. Got 2 go wiv Enid 2 hspital on Fri. I put in diary. Meat wagon cumin at 10.

Fortunately, most reports are completed on computer nowadays, so spellchecker is available. However, every effort should be used to avoid jargon and to use complete sentences. Having good keyboard skills is always an advantage.

Emails are a reliable, cheap and quick type of communication between health care professionals. The advantage of an email over a telephone call is that a record of the conversation can be kept and referred back to.

BARRIERS TO COMMUNICATION

THE COMMUNICATION CYCLE

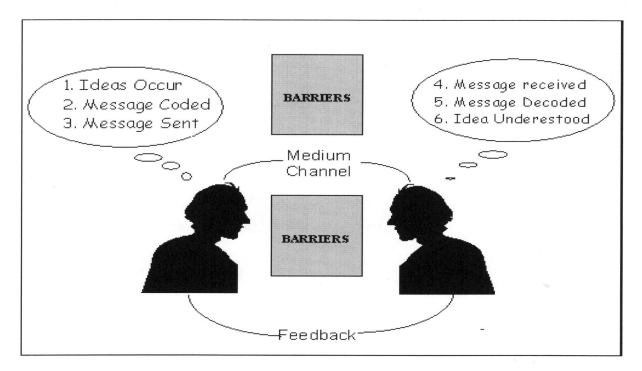

In order to communicate you have to go through a process with another person. This process is called the communication cycle because the process goes round in a circle.

Ideas occur – you think of something you want to communicate. Communication always has a purpose. It might be to pass on information or an idea, or to persuade someone to do something, or to entertain or inspire.

Message coded – you think about how you are going to say what you are thinking and decide in what form the communication will be, for example, spoken word or sign language. You put it into this form in your head.

Message sent – you send the message, for example speak or sign what you want to communicate.

Message received – the other person senses that you have sent a message by, for example, hearing your words or seeing your signs.

Message decoded – the other person has to interpret what you have communicated; this is known as decoding.

Message understood – if you have communicated clearly and the other person has concentrated, and there are no barriers to communication, the other person understands your ideas. They show this by giving you feedback, i.e. by sending you a message back.

THINGS THAT CAN WRONG

The person who has the first idea may not make the meaning clear and might assume that the other person is ready and willing to listen to them when they are not. They might also assume that the other person has heard what they said properly and has not been distracted by something else they are interested in. They might have used terms and language that the other person is unfamiliar with or might have started half way through a story assuming that they already knew the beginning. This can lead to the other person making assumptions as to what they meant, jumping to conclusions and so leading them to talk at cross purposes.

Have you ever been in the situation where you have said something to someone and they haven't heard all of what you have said?

Here's an example:

Graham: Hey! Did you hear that Sammy from down the pub has broken his arm?

Sally: Ummm?

Graham: He fell of his motorbike. It's in plaster.

Sally: His motorbike's in plaster? Why?

FACTORS THAT EFFECT COMMUNICATION

Some things prevent communication being effective. For example, if the television is on and you are speaking to a person who has hearing problems, they might not be able to hear you clearly. The television is the barrier to effective communication. People who work in a health or social care environment need to understand the barriers so they can overcome them.

It is very important to be able to communicate effectively in a health or social care setting. The client cannot fully participate if they cannot hear what is being said or understand what is being communicated. In the same way, the care professional cannot fully assess and meet the client's needs if the client is prevented from communicating effectively.

BARRIERS TO COMMUNICATION

Sensory Deprivation

Loss or partial loss of sight, hearing, touch, smell and taste can cause barriers to communication.

Foreign Language

People who do not speak English as a first language may find this a barrier to effective communication.

Environmental Factors

Dark rooms, proximity of chairs, loud noises, traffic or train sounds all make communication difficult

Jargon

Sometimes, health professionals use medical terms that are not understood by the client

Distress

People who are distressed often don't communicate well or understand what is being said to them

Education

Poor levels of education can make written communication difficult

Cultural Differences

Making eye contact is considered impolite I some cultures.

Health Issues

People, who are feeling ill, often don't want to communicate in any great depth.

Aggressive Behaviour

If a client becomes aggressive, it is difficult to communicate with them.

Lack of Aids

Lack of aids to effective communication such as hearing aids or interpreters

ACTIVITY 9

In this activity you will suggest some barriers to communication that might be seen in the health and social care workplace. Write them into the first column. In the second column, suggest ways to overcome these barriers

BARRIER TO COMMUNICATION	WAYS TO OVERCOME IT

WAYS TO OVERCOME BARRIERS TO COMMUNICATION

Verbal skills to overcome barriers

When you use your verbal skills effectively, you can help overcome barriers that might be preventing effective communication. Let's have a look at a few of these tactics.

Paraphrasing means repeating back something a person has just said in a different way to make sure you have understood the message.

For example, someone says, 'I've had this pain since Monday' and you may respond by saying, 'So you had this pain for four days?'

Closed questions are questions that can be answered with either a single word or short phrase, for example, 'Can you walk at all?' could be answered, 'No' or, 'Not very far.' Closed questions give facts, they are easy and quick to answer but they don't give much in the way of detailed information

They are useful as an opening question, such as 'Are you feeling better?' and for ending a conversation, such as, 'Are you happy with the progress we have made today?'

Open questions are questions that require a longer answer, for example, 'Why don't you like sprouts?' might be answered by, 'I haven't liked the taste or smell of them since I was made to eat them all the time when I was a child...'.

Open questions hand control of the conversation to the person you are speaking to. They ask the person to think and reflect, give opinions and feelings. They are useful as a follow-up to a closed question, to find out more, to help someone realise or face their problems and to show concern about them.

Clarification means to make something clear and understandable. Summarising means to sum up what has been said in a short, clear way.

ADAPTING THE ENVIRONMENT

This can be done in a number of ways, such as improving lighting for those with sight impairments and reducing background noise for those with hearing impairments. Lifts can be installed with a voice giving information such as when the doors are opening and closing and which floor the lift is on for those who can't see. Ramps can be added, reception desks lowered and signs put lower down on walls, so that people with physical disabilities can access the people and information they need.

We also looked at other methods of adapting the environment earlier.

Can you remember what they were? Write three more ways to adapt the environment to aid effective communication in the space below.

_____

_____

_____

ACTIVITY 10

Look at the picture above. It is taken in the lounge of a residential care home.

Questions:
1. What effect do you think the physical layout of the room might have on communication between residents? Explain your answer clearly.

2. How do you think residents' would feel about sitting in this room? Why? What effect could staying in this room for long periods have on their self-esteem?

3. Draw a plan of an alternative layout for the lounge in the space below. You must include 15 chairs and a television, but can add other (non-luxury) items or pieces of furniture if you wish. Focus mainly on how the chairs should be positioned to help communication, but still allow movement around the room.

RECORD KEEPING

Why do we keep records?

Records and reports have a huge impact on the lives of the people you care for. They are important documents that remain with a person through their life and are an opportunity to communicate essential information to ensure their care, health, safety and welfare needs are met.

List 3 documents you are expected to complete within your role e.g. care plan, daily notes, food and drink, medication administration records, risk assessments, accident or incident form, complaints, diary etc

Document	What information is available to you in this document?	What could happen to a person you care for and support if you did not have this information?

Records help provide consistency in care, treatment and support – they help to protect people, maintain their dignity and allow opportunities to 'live' and take positive risks.

THE CARE PROFESSIONAL'S ROLE IN KEEPING RECORDS

The General Social Care Council code of practice Standard 6.2 states that as a social care worker you are expected to:

'Maintain clear and accurate records as required by procedures established by your work'.

The care organisation will have policies and procedures that relate to record keeping. These policies and procedures will abide by the Data Protection Act 1998.

ACTIVITY 11

Using the internet as a research tool, wright a paragraph to explain the main points of the Data Protection Act 1998

Records are legal documents which means you have to stand by what you write in them. This is why you are expected to sign and date them. You must be able to explain every statement you make because you could be asked about it in a court of law. In the eyes of the Law, if information is not recorded it did not happen - so you would not be able to rely on saying that you passed the information on verbally to a senior member of staff if you have not recorded it.

BEST PRACICE IN RECORD WRITING

Personal records need to be legible and readable as well as:

Understandable – the words you use need to be clear and simple. Sentences need to be short and you must try not to use abbreviations or jargon

Relevant – Keep to the point; focus on the reason for the record.

Clear and concise – Think about what you would need to know if you were the next person reading this record and you needed the key information quickly.

Factual and checkable – the reason for this is because everyone looking after this person relies on the records to help them make important decisions. If records are inaccurate, mistakes may be made. Records also provide a mass of detail no one person could possibly remember. Records need to be signed and dated.

Non-judgemental – you are reporting events not opinions or your perception of something or someone.

It is also important to make sure the language and tone are respectful and positive
Watch out for language that could Show disrespect – being 'naughty', 'uncooperative', 'going on and on about it'

Be 'vague' – a general description that has no specific meaning 'gets aggressive', 'slept well', 'challenging behaviour', 'quiet day'

Suggest a stereotype – 'typical Down's syndrome', 'the disabled', 'the elderly', 'diabetic'. Any label that conveys a general attitude towards a group of people and does not acknowledge them as an individual

It so important to keep accurate records so everyone knows what is happening and what they should be doing. They provide key information on which to build relationships with the people you care for and support. These documents are a permanent record of a person's life whilst they are living in a care organisation or home.
They provide evidence that something happened as it should e.g. medication administration records. They also show 'who did what and when'.
You can refer back to the records if you forget something or need to find something out. So everyone has the same message/information.
If the worst were to happen and something went wrong with the support someone received they would be a vital source of information.

WRITING DAILY RECORDS

Read the following two extracts from a daily record.

18 th	Quiet day. Assisted to wash and dress. No problems.	BE
19/th	Slept well. Medication given.	AN
20 th	Had breakfast. D/N visited.	KC
	Weighed this afternoon then took part in activities. Had a good night. Woke a few times but otherwise slept well. GP visited.	
21 st	Had a bath then assisted to dress. Sat in lounge. Had a visitor this afternoon. Spent the evening in bedroom.	BE
	Asleep on all checks. No problems.	
	No problems this morning. All usual care given.	

Would you know from this record:

- Who was being written about?
- What his or her pain levels were like?
- What activities they had participated in
- If their leg ulcer was healing or not?
- Whether they slept well or not?
- Who had written the report?

19/04/2013 10.30am	Vera told me she thoroughly enjoyed her cooked breakfast. We chatted about life on the farm while I assisted her with her personal hygiene.	Helen B
3.30pm	She decided she wanted to stay in her room for the morning but joined her friends at lunchtime in the dining room. Vera had a snooze after lunch then played cards. She celebrated her win by sharing her prize – box of chocolates - with other residents.	Helen B
10pm	Vera spent the evening in her room watching television and knitting. Vera wanted an early night so I gave her medication and helped her settle into bed around 9pm.	Sheila H
20/04/201 6.30am	Vera woke around 5.30 this morning for her early morning cup of tea. Vera said she had slept well although her shoulders were very stiff. She did not want the pain relief I offered.	Betty K
11.00am	After breakfast Vera said she wanted to wash on her own today but called me to assist with putting on her clothes as her shoulders were quite painful. I asked if she would like any pain relief or to see her GP and Vera said she would like to see the doctor tomorrow if her shoulders haven't improved. Senior carer (Lucy Willis) informed. The District Nurse visited and has removed the dressing from Vera's leg as the ulcer is now finally healed. Vera told her it was	Helen B

	because of all the 'wonderful' food she had to eat in here and mentioned how she had lost interest in cooking for herself after her husband died last Summer. Vera talked a little about her husband and became upset. She said she was able to cry now because she didn't have to be 'strong' and find a way to keep the farm going.	
3.50pm	Vera cheered up this afternoon when I weighed her as she has put on 4 lbs over the 3 weeks since she has been living here. Vera tried out watercolour painting for the first time today and said she had no ideas she could learn something new at her age!	Helen B
	Vera found it very difficult to get comfortable this evening due to the pain in her shoulders. Pain medication offered but refused.	
	She woke several times requesting Paracetamol which was given at 21.00 to settle, then at 02.30 and 07.00.	

After reading the second report, you should be able to identify the differences between this one and the first one.

ACTIVITY 12

In pairs make a list of all the positive things and negative things about both of the reports. Then compare your answers with the rest of the class.

	Positives	Negatives
1st Report		
2nd Report		

RECORDS IN THE HEALTH AND SOCIAL CARE SETTING

Not all records that are kept on a client are in report format. Sometimes they are in chart format or presented as a grid to fill in.

A Medication Administration record is often referred to as a MAR sheet. Each client has their own record sheet with details of their prescribed medication on it. It allows the care professional to record the date and time the medication was given, who gave it and any other notes that are needed. It is an accurate and legal document that could be used in a court of law if anything when wrong.

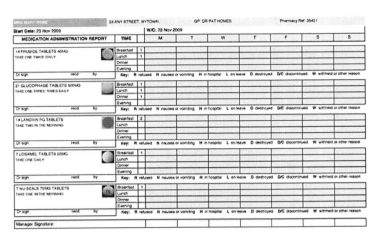

Another type of record might be a fluid balance chart which records the amount of all the fluids that the clients has drunk or been given intravenously. It also records all amounts of urine passed throughout the day. This record is especially important for clients who have kidney dysfunction.

YORK HEALTH SERVICES
NHS TRUST
FLUID BALANCE CHART   DATE..........................
ORAL/N-G FLUID ORDERS

INPUT (ml)				OUTPUT (ml)					
TIME	ORAL/NG	N/S IV	m/ml IV	IV	VOMIT/ ASPIRATE	OTHER STATE	OTHER STATE	OTHER STATE	URINE	TEST
14:00	100	1000	100ml							
15:00									300	
16:00	150				25				150	
17:00										
18:00	350		50ml						400	
19:00										
20:00										
21:00	150									
22:00			100ml							
23:00									430	
24:00										
01:00										
02:00										
03:00										
04:00		1000								
05:00										
06:00			100ml							
07:00	150								375	
08:00	300				130					
09:00									485	
10:00	150								150	
11:00										
12:00	120								350	
13:00		200							150	
SUB TOTALS										

TOTAL INPUT = _____ ml.   TOTAL OUTPUT = _____ ml.
DAILY BALANCE = _____

WPG 253

QUESTIONS

1. Explain why it is important to keep these type of records up to date

_____
_____
_____
_____
_____
_____

2. Explain how a person <u>without</u> training might complete these kinds of records incorrectly.

_____
_____
_____
_____
_____
_____

3. Which law applies to the keeping of these types of records.

_____

4. Describe how these kinds of records could be used in a case of negligence.

_____
_____
_____
_____
_____

Well Done!

You have now completed your course.

Printed in Great Britain
by Amazon.co.uk, Ltd.,
Marston Gate.